Hygge Day

Cute and Cozy Coloring Book for Adults and Teens with Simple Designs of Super Cute Animals for Relaxation

Thank you for your purchase!

If you have time, kindly leave a review, if you're happy with your purchase!

Color Test Page

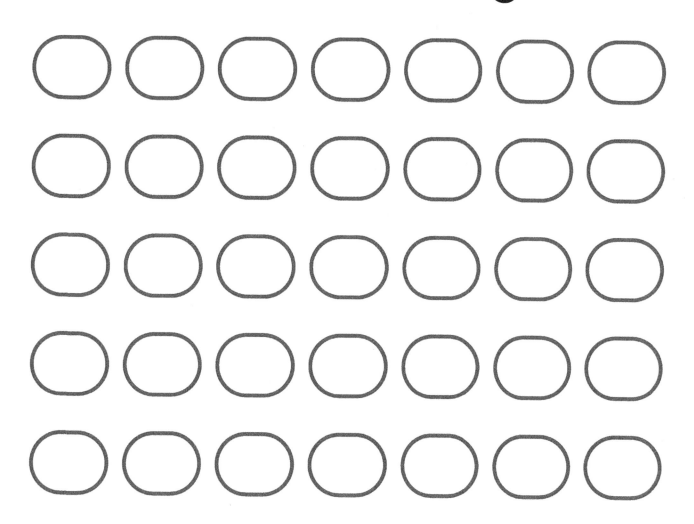

Quick Tip!

If using markers, it's recommended that you place a blank sheet
of paper behind the page to prevent any bleed-through.

Made in the USA
Las Vegas, NV
12 October 2024